Make a Marionette

by Lynne Anderson

Table of Contents

What Is a Marionette?

Have you read or seen the story
of Pinocchio? If so, then you already
know what a marionette is. A marionette
is a puppet that is moved from above
by strings, wires, or rods.

▲ People have been enjoying marionettes
for hundreds of years.

Marionettes are usually small human or animal figures. They are used to tell a story on a stage. A person behind the stage makes the marionette move. This person is called a puppeteer.

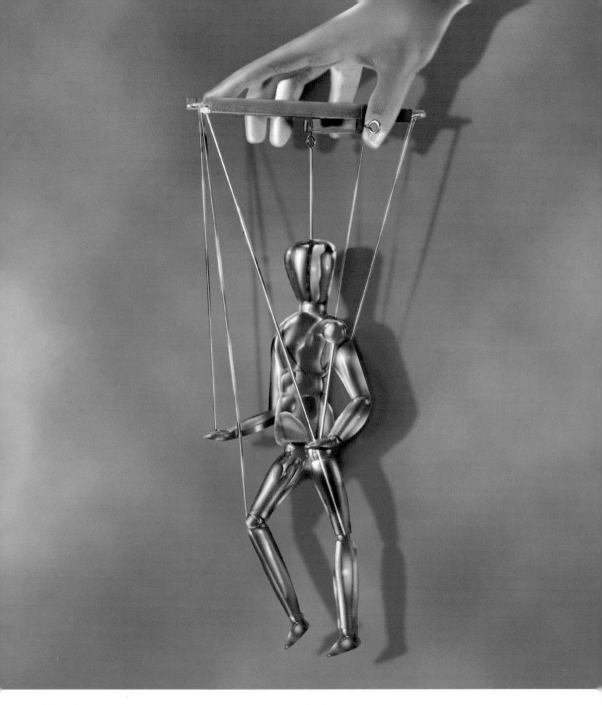

▲ The puppeteer raises and lowers a marionette's wires or strings to make it move.

How Can You Make a Marionette?

You can make your own marionette.
Just follow the steps on these pages.

Here is what you will need:

1 sock

yarn

1 glove

scissors

cotton

4 safety pins

2 rubber bands

2 ice-cream sticks

markers

cloth or paper

Step 1 First put some cotton in the toe of the sock. This will be the marionette's head. Put a rubber band below the head to make a neck.

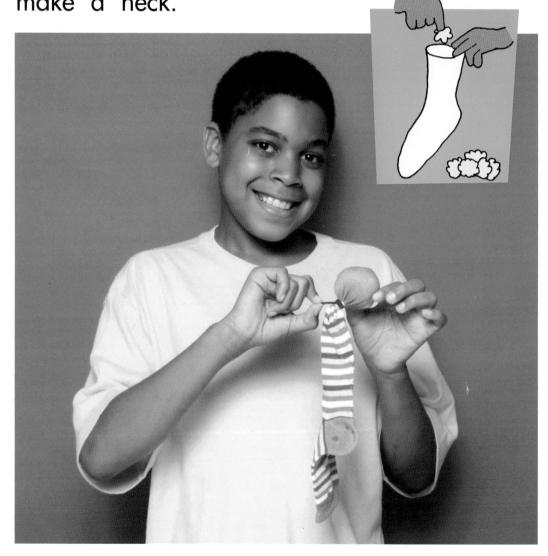

Now put cotton in the rest of the sock. This will be the body. Put a rubber band around the bottom of the body. Cut off any extra sock.

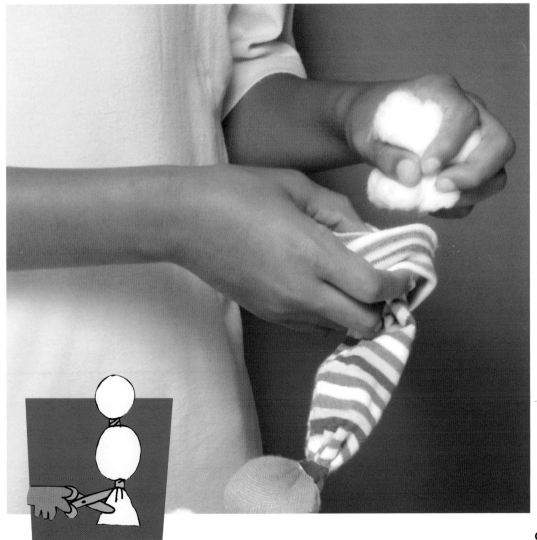

Step 3 Use markers to give the marionette a face. You should draw eyes, a nose, and a mouth.

 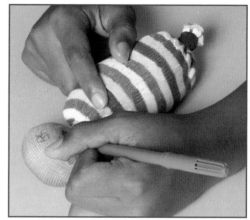

Step 4 Next, cut strips of yarn. Glue them on for hair.

Step 5 Then cut off the fingers of the glove.

 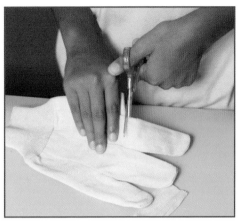

Step 6 Put cotton into two of the fingers to make arms. Stuff the other two fingers to make legs.

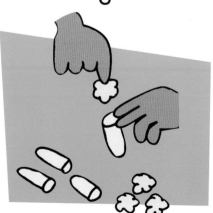 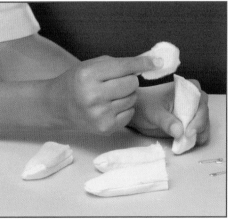

Step 7 Put two spots on the body where you want the arms to go. Then mark where you want the legs to go. Ask an adult helper to pin the arms and the legs in place with the safety pins.

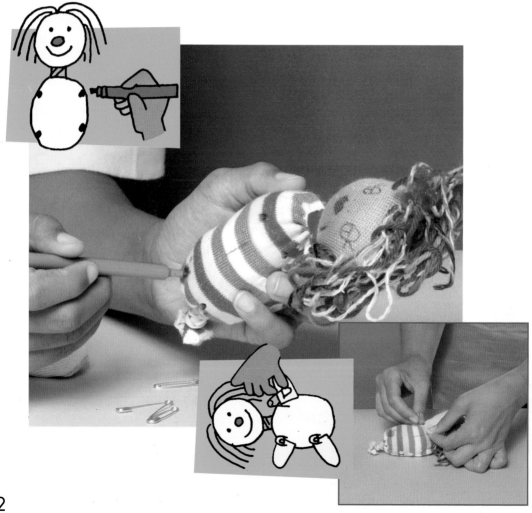

Step 8 Give the marionette some clothes. You can use cloth or paper.

Step 9 Cut two pieces of yarn. They should be the length from your elbow to your fingertips.

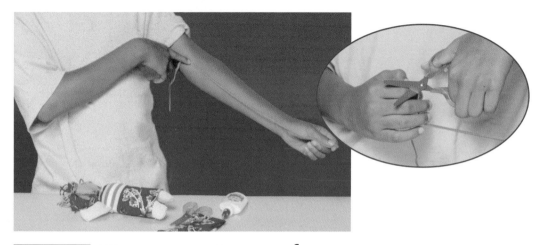

Step 10 Tie one piece of yarn to each arm. Tie the free ends of the yarn to an ice-cream stick.

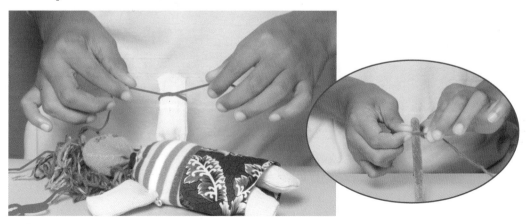

Step 11 Cut two more pieces of yarn. These pieces should be the length from your shoulder to your fingertips.

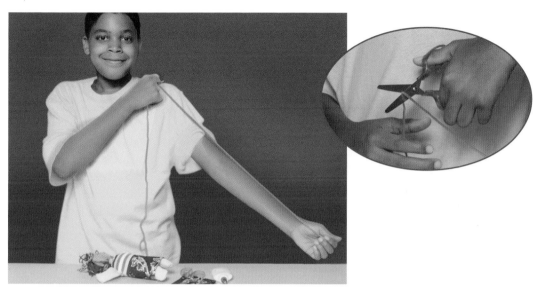

Step 12 Tie one piece of yarn to each leg. Tie the free ends of the yarn to the other ice-cream stick.

Step 13 Hold one stick in each hand and try to make your marionette move. Can you make your marionette dance?